Look, It's Snowing!

By Clem King

Contents

Fun When It Snows

I have the best time when it snows.

Look outside!

I can see snow!

You can enjoy the snow
if you put on warm things.

Pull a big wool sock onto
each foot.

Pull on a fuzzy wool hat.

Put on a big coat
with a hood, too.

Fun in the Snow

This man took his dog out in the snow.

They played and jumped in the snow.

But then the dog played
in the snow!

It shook lots of snow
high and low.

Fun Inside

You can bake cookies
when it snows.

You can dip the cookies
in hot milk!

I like to cook a jam pudding.

I put all the things in a dish.

I mix it up!

Dad puts a mitt on
to get the hot pudding.

I eat lots of pudding
and feel **so** full.

Then I sit and read
a good book.

I pull my wool rug
onto my legs.

Mum and Dad push big bits
of wood onto the flames.

We put nuts in a pan
and enjoy the good smell!

But look out for soot!

Soot can put black spots
on your things.

soot

It's so good when it snows.

You can cook, read a book
or just look outside!

CHECKING FOR MEANING

1. What are some of the warm things to wear in the snow that are shown in the book? *(Literal)*

2. Who took the hot pudding out of the oven? *(Literal)*

3. Why might wearing a hood in the snow be a good idea? *(Inferential)*

EXTENDING VOCABULARY

fuzzy	What does something look like if it is *fuzzy*? What does it feel like? What can be fuzzy besides a wool hat?
pudding	What is a *pudding*? What do you need to make a pudding? What flavours of pudding have you had?
soot	What is *soot*? Explain that soot is a black powder that forms from burnt wood. What other words can you think of that rhyme with *soot*?

MOVING BEYOND THE TEXT

1. What are some sports that people play in the snow?

2. Do you like cold weather or warm weather? Why?

3. What are some other foods that are good to eat when it is cold?

4. Where in the world does it snow a lot?

DIPHTHONGS

| oy | ow | oo | aw |

PRACTICE WORDS

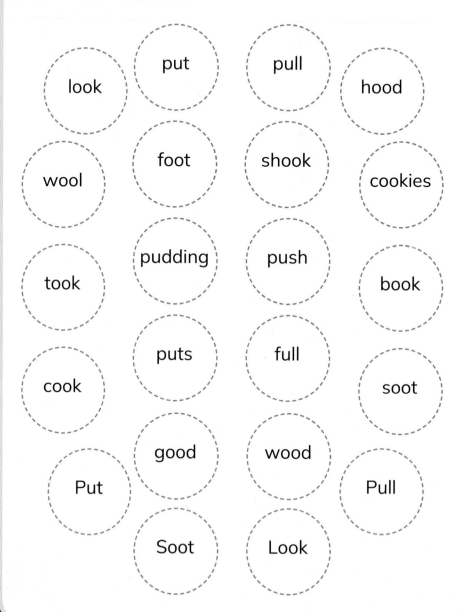

look

put

pull

hood

wool

foot

shook

cookies

took

pudding

push

book

cook

puts

full

soot

Put

good

wood

Pull

Soot

Look